人咸知其真
不飾哉

Written by Joëlle Busuttil
Illustrated by Laurence Quentin

Specialist adviser:
Sean Sheehan B.A., P.G.C.E.

ISBN 1 85103 171 5
First published 1993 in the United Kingdom
by Moonlight Publishing Ltd,
36 Stratford Road, London W8
Translated by Sarah Matthews

Printed in Italy by Editoriale Libraria

Living in China

One quarter of all the people
living in the world
are Chinese.

THE HUMAN WORLD

Peasants carry vegetables, and even live ducks, in wicker baskets balanced on their bicycles or slung on bamboo poles.

More people live in China than in any other country in the world.

There are more than one billion two hundred million people living in China. The capital of China is Beijing. As early as six o'clock in the morning, crowds begin to fill the streets. Pedlars are everywhere selling their goods and services, one offering to repair your bike, another to clean your ears...

There is every imaginable kind of landscape in China: plains, mountains, deserts...
And not everyone who lives there is Chinese.

Tibetans, Manchus and Mongols also live in China, but the Chinese outnumber them all. The other peoples are ethnic minorities.

The Dalai Lama, the living god of the Tibetans, lived in the Potala, on the roof of the world, 7,000 metres above sea level.

The nomads of Mongolia herd their horses and put up their yurts, tents of skin or felt, out on the frozen plains.

In southern China, rice grown on terraces is harvested two or three times a year.

The Huang River (5,000 km long) floods often, and is called the Scourge of China. The Yangtze (5,800 km long) is safer.

In the tropical south of China, with palm trees and bamboo thickets, water buffalo help the peasants to till the rice fields.

The oasis of Turpan, in the middle of the north-eastern deserts, is famous for its beautiful Muslim mosque.

Eastwards, the Great Wall goes right down on to the sandy beaches of the Yellow Sea.

The Great Wall of China is so large that it can be seen from the Moon!

Building work was started on the Wall in 200 BC by the Emperor Qin Shi Huangdi, who wanted to keep out barbarian invaders coming in from the north.

One thousand seven hundred years later, the Wall was over 3,000 kilometres long. People said that each stone of the Wall had been paid for with a human life. Today, the Great Wall still stands along the northern hills of China. Part of it has been restored so that tourists can walk along it.

This huge citadel stands at the western end of the Wall. It is the biggest fortress in the world.

The emperors of China used to live in the Forbidden City, in the heart of the city of Beijing.

Nobody was allowed into the Forbidden City except for the emperor, his family, and all his servants. The City was enclosed by moats and by a huge wall over ten metres high. Inside the wall were enormous squares and gardens, eight hundred palaces, with nine thousand different rooms!

The buildings of the Forbidden City had roofs made of tiles varnished in bright yellow, the imperial colour.

Pu Yi was just two years old when he became the last emperor of China in 1908. His later years were spent working as a gardener in the Forbidden City.

The emperors' throne was decorated in yellow and gold. It stood in a room called the Room of Heavenly Peace. When a prince became emperor he was called the Son of Heaven. It was a crime to speak his name.

The most important ceremonies were held in the square outside the imperial palace: the coronation of the emperor, and celebrations of the New Year and of emperors' birthdays.

People's Republic

In 1949, the Chinese communists took over the running of China, under the leadership of Mao Zedong, the Chairman of the new republic. He was a powerful ruler and was regarded as a great hero. His ideas are not so popular now, but they still shape the way China is run.

A stamp showing the head of Chairman Mao

Mao published his ideas in a small, red book. The Little Red Book sold over 800 million copies.

The body of Mao Zedong was embalmed and placed on public view in a mausoleum in Tiananmen Square.

China is a great power.

It is also a very poor country. The millions of people need great quantities of food, clothing and machinery. In many places, work done by machines in the West is done by hand. It is a slow, uncertain business to modernize such a vast country. But nearly everyone in China has a job, and the Chinese sell more food and products abroad than they have to import.

Over nine million people live in Beijing.

The city sprawls over 40 kilometres. In winter the temperature can drop to -20 degrees centigrade, while in spring dust blows in from the Gobi Desert to cover the city.

The symbol of Tiananmen Square: the big star stands for the communist party, the other four stand for the working class, the peasant class, the middle class and the upper middle class. Tiananmen Square is the largest square in the world.

There are many beautiful cities in China.

Suzhou, with its hundreds of canals, is called the Venice of China. It stands on the Grand Canal, which joins the Yangtze River to Beijing. Marco Polo, a visitor who came to China from Venice in the fourteenth century, was particularly fascinated by Suzhou.

The Chinese love birds, and will often go for walks carrying their caged birds with them.

In Shanghai, a huge port and industrial centre, you can go and have tea in tea-houses which stand on piles driven into the water.

Tea is the national drink of China.

The usual tea is green tea, which you can buy in small, individual packets.
The Chinese drink tea at any hour of the day and night, but they don't add milk or sugar.

A tea-house in Shanghai

There are more pigs in China than in any other country in the world.

Eight of every ten Chinese people live in the country.

In central and southern China, rice is the most important crop. The peasants work in the paddy-fields in their bare feet, up to their ankles in water. They wear big, flat hats on their heads to protect them from the sun. In the north-east, they grow wheat, millet and sorghum. But much of the land in China is no good for growing things, and so what good land there is must be used as well as possible. Even in the cities, people will keep chickens to help feed their families. Fish farms, particularly carp farms, provide another source of food.

An outdoor restaurant in Beijing. The food is steamed in baskets piled one on top of the other.

In southern China, most people eat rice at every meal.

In the north, though, they prefer bread rolls or noodles made with egg and flour. When Marco Polo visited China he discovered these noodles, and took some back to Italy with him. The Italians liked them so much that pasta soon became the national dish. The Chinese do not use butter or cheese. All the fresh milk is saved for the children. Grown-ups drink soya milk, which is made from soya beans. They often finish a meal with soup.

Food is cut up into small chunks, and eaten with chopsticks.

It's not easy to eat with chopsticks! Both sticks are held in one hand, but only one stick moves up and down. The Chinese like to drink hot water. A thermos of boiled water is kept for drinking and making tea.

Chinese dishes: noodles, hundred-year eggs, shark fins, black mushrooms, roast duck, steamed buns, ginger...

What do Chinese houses look like?

Traditional Chinese houses have a central open courtyard. In the past just one family lived in each house, but now several families share each building. In cities, most people live in high-rise flats.

Many Chinese do Tai Chi, special exercises, with or without a stick. It looks as though they are fighting an enemy in slow motion.

Because the living space for each family can be small, most family life goes on outdoors. First thing in the morning, people do their Tai Chi in the streets, on their own or in groups. In the evenings, parks and pavements are crowded with people taking a walk, talking to friends, playing board games. It is difficult to be alone in China.

Grandmothers take babies for walks in their bamboo prams. They do not use nappies in China: the babies wear trousers with an open seam to leave their bottoms bare, even in winter.

There are lots of modern houses in China, but often a whole family lives in just one room.

Family life

Every year the number of people in China increases by about 12 million. Only 15% of China's land can produce food, so it is a problem trying to feed everyone. This is why the government urges couples to have only one child each. It is very common these days for a Chinese child to be an only child.

Schools

Schools are very crowded. Children have only had to go to school since 1985. Many people have never been taught to read and write. For country families, it may seem more important for children to work in the fields, helping to bring in food for the family.

How do people get about in China?

Most people travel by bicycle. There are still very few cars. Peasants use carts pulled by donkeys to take their fruit and vegetables to market. The buses are always packed full of people, and they can only move very slowly through the crowds of cyclists!

What does Chinese writing look like?

The Chinese do not use an alphabet like we do. Each word is made up of just one or two characters. These characters are like little drawings. They are called ideograms. You need to know at least three thousand separate characters to be able to read a newspaper. An educated Chinese will know at least six thousand. The characters each have a 'key' which gives some idea of what the word means. There are 214 keys. Chinese dictionaries put groups of words together under each key.

人
man

日
sun

月
moon

水
water

火
fire

山
mountain

To sign their calligraphies and their paintings, the Chinese use a seal carved with their name.

Chinese writing is very beautiful.

The Chinese take great pride in learning to write as beautifully as possible. They write using a brush and very black ink which they make themselves from an ink-stone onto which they drip a little bit of water.

This special writing is called calligraphy.

An abacus makes it possible to do sums very quickly. Most shop assistants use them.

一	二	三	四	五	六	七	八	九	十
1	2	3	4	5	6	7	8	9	10

The panda is the national symbol of China.

Pandas live in bamboo forests. They eat just one type of bamboo, and there are not many pandas left. These huge black and white bears are extremely strong and have long, razor-sharp claws. A fully grown panda can weigh over a hundred kilos.

Statues are carved in the shapes of different animals.

For the Chinese, different animals stand for different things: elephants for wisdom, tortoises for long life, grasshoppers for immortality. Lions are good for protecting people from harm.

This stone lion is guarding the house.

The New Year is the most important festival in China.

It is celebrated somewhere between our 21st January and our 19th February. The date changes every year. On New Year's Day, people let off fireworks and bangers to chase away the evil spirits.

The Beijing Opera is very popular.

There are operas all year round, and seats are cheap. The words are spoken or sung. Each opera can last for several hours, and people come and go, seeing just a part, or all of it, depending on how much time they have.

A dragon dance to celebrate the New Year

Each actor in an opera wears different make-up according to the character they are playing. They move very slowly and gracefully, using their hands and arms as much as their voices.

The symbol of yin and yang represents the union of opposites.

This Taoist monk is burning incense.

The Chinese are great inventors.

They invented the first compass, the first cross-bow, the first gunpowder, the first paper, the first pasta...

There are two great Chinese religions: Taoism and Buddhism.

To sum them up in a few words, you could say Taoists believe that everything is a balance between yin and yang, male and female, hot and cold, inside and outside...

Buddhists believe that by self-discipline and effort a person may gain insight, wisdom and eventually perfect enlightenment, called nirvana.

Buddha was a wise Indian monk. His teachings spread all over the Far East.

Would you like to be able to tell your fortune according to Chinese astrology?

The year in which you were born matches one of the twelve signs of the Chinese zodiac. Don't forget that the Chinese New Year starts at the end of January. The different animals associated with each year all have different characters. Rats are supposed to be cunning, buffaloes calm, tigers daring, rabbits happy, dragons lucky, serpents intuitive, horses enthusiastic, goats artistic, monkeys curious, roosters lively, dogs faithful and pigs generous! Which are you?

Rat 1924-1936-1948-1960-1972-1984

Tiger 1926-1938-1950-1962-1974-1986

Buffalo 1925-1937-1949-1961-1973-1985

Rabbit 1927-1939-1951-1963-1975-1987

Dragon 1928-1940-1952-1964-1976-1988

Serpent 1929-1941-1953-1965-1977-1989

Horse 1930-1942-1954-1966-1978-1990

Goat 1931-1943-1955-1967-1979-1991

Monkey 1932-1944-1956-1968-1980-1992

Rooster 1933-1945-1957-1969-1981-1993

Dog 1934-1946-1958-1970-1982-1994

Pig 1935-1947-1959-1971-1983-1995

Index